a secret
garden

a secret
garden

annie bullen

Publication in this form copyright © Jarrold Publishing 2004
Text copyright © Jarrold Publishing
The moral right of the author has been asserted
Series editor Jenni Davis
Designed by Mark Buckingham
Photography by Neil Jinkerson,
except pages 12, 56, 57, 64, 76

Thanks to poet Toby Rivas, who wrote *The Window Box*
on page 56 especially for this book.
All efforts were made to trace other copyright holders but without success.
The publishers will be pleased to rectify any omissions in future editions.

The front cover picture was taken at Rookwoods, Gloucestershire,
courtesy of Mr and Mrs Des Althorp; the back cover picture was taken at
The Little Cottage, Hampshire, courtesy of Peter and Lyn Prior.

A CIP catalogue for this book is available from the British Library.

Published by:
Jarrold Publishing
Healey House, Dene Road, Andover, Hampshire, SP10 2AA
www.britguides.com

Set in Bembo
Printed in Singapore
ISBN 1 84165 140 0   1/04

Pitkin is an imprint of Jarrold Publishing, Norwich

contents

introduction

White fantail doves and wooden garden seats are traditional ingredients of secret gardens.

There's an old saying that tells you to take a lover to secure short-term bliss, while the traditional recipe for a few more years of joy is to get married. But if you want your whole lifetime to be filled with happiness and contentment you should plant a garden.

There's something in that. Plants obey natural cycles and you must contain your impatience and learn to fall back into step with the rhythms of the earth.

Be inspired to grow your own secret garden, using the plants and materials that most appeal to you, and be content to watch it grow, beautifully, over the years.

why create a secret garden?

The pleasure of entering a garden is heightened if you can't see everything at once. Curving paths help to prolong the sense of anticipation.

'I'm going to live for ever and ever and ever!' shouted young Colin, as the magic of a secret garden struck his soul, changing him from a crabbed, sickly and spoilt child to a creature at one with the world.

Colin Craven and his cousin Mary Lennox, two lonely and unloved children, respond to the miracle of burgeoning green life hidden inside the old brick walls of Frances Hodgson Burnett's much-loved children's classic, *The Secret Garden.*

The writer knew that most of us will lose ourselves in the constantly renewing cycle of nature. Plants and trees grow, without our attention. We can build something beautiful by shaping nature, but, left to its own devices, a garden will show a certain character, create its own atmosphere, before it becomes a wild tangle, waiting for the kiss of the gardener's

shears, the touch of a fork or spade to tame and shape it once more.

Our own secret gardens may be nothing more than a tranquil corner with a tree-shaded seat, a tiny pool, a pot full of plants sown and raised over months. They may be grander, with doorways, gates, paths, roses, sculpture. But once we care for a garden with a life of its own, anger and resentment about the world outside quickly drain away as we lose ourselves in our own green and secret place.

'It was the sweetest, most mysterious-looking place anyone could imagine.'

Frances Hodgson Burnett,
The Secret Garden

'The world is too much with us; late and soon,
Getting and spending, we lay waste our powers:
Little we see in Nature that is ours.'

William Wordsworth, *The World is Too Much With Us*

We all hold a place within our hearts that can be reached by a sight, a sound, a smell; something that makes us vulnerable because it is outside our will to close the way in to that place.

It would be quite wrong to confuse vulnerability with weakness. Allowing

ourselves to be moved by something that has no direct bearing on things or people we want to possess is liberating and we should be able to recognize the peace and contentment that inspires.

Enjoy that bit of you that is moved by the sight of an empty chair under a tree, a thin trickle of water over pebbles or old stone, the lemony scent of sun-warmed honeysuckle. It is yours alone, unless and until you invite someone to share your pleasure. That is how secret gardens are made.

A glorious froth of
Hydrangea arborescens
Annabelle provides an
unexpected underplanting.

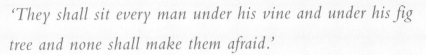

'*They shall sit every man under his vine and under his fig tree and none shall make them afraid.*'

Micah IV, v.4

How often do gardeners sit down to enjoy their creation? You sit, consider – and bounce up to pull out a weed, trim a patch of untidy grass, dead-head the roses, collect some seed. Somehow you can't help yourself. Simply sitting is a peaceful pleasure denied to most gardeners by their own urge to polish what is already perfect. You make a secret garden to change all that.

A secret garden is the place where you can allow straight edges to become blurred, soft tangles to creep into the flower beds, scented herbs to seed gently about. It's a place for collections of stones, garden ornaments that appeal to you alone, a path overhung with unconfined flowers, a seat.

That seat is to be used. Tuck it away if you will – under an apple tree, inside a hedge, beneath a leafy arbour – but make sure your bench or chair is where you want it to be. Furnish it with a few soft cushions and your favourite books, whatever it takes to turn the garden into a place that makes you the mistress or master rather than the slave.

A seat is an essential element of a secret garden.

13

A garden may be 'secret' because of its position, perhaps tucked away in unexpected surroundings. Opening a door in a high fence or wall running alongside a busy main road and coming across a perfectly enclosed garden within, where you least expect it, is an extraordinary experience.

For just a moment you can't speak; you don't trust your senses. Behind you is tarmac and concrete and metal and noise and fumes. Close the door and another world enfolds you. The clipped green hedges muffle the rumble and thump of traffic; a neat line of potted topiary – perfect rounds of standard euonymus or triangles of box – draws your eye to a seat tucked away under a shady green ivy arbour. Brick paths define the edges of borders filled to overflowing with delicate yellow coreopsis, deep blue salvias and white scabious. What could be a better secret than one designed to delight and jolt all the senses into a new reality?

Clipped green trees, brick paths and blue, white and lemon flowers give a feeling of perfect peace in this enclosed town garden.

'*Annihilating all that's made*
To a green thought in a
green shade.'

Andrew Marvell,
Thoughts in a Garden

Loops of thick rope make interesting supports for climbing or rambling roses.

The classic secret garden is enclosed, full of flowers and fruit, lovingly planned and worked – before being abandoned. Frances Hodgson Burnett's walled garden was deliberately locked, the door concealed and the key hidden because a beloved wife had died there in a tragic accident.

A 20th-century example is the Lost Garden of Heligan in Cornwall, where a wonderful Victorian garden, once belonging to the Tremayne family, lay hidden beneath the wild over-growth

of decades. The incredible story of its restoration is a well-known one and now it is secret no more, although today's gardeners can be inspired by the many secrets it has given up.

These are two evocative and magical stories of romance and discovery.

It is not necessary to have acres of land to create a secret garden. Claim a corner of the family patch and make it yours with water, a seat, a fence or a hedge. Plant herbs for their scent or roses for that touch of romance. Copy the grand French gardens and loop a thick rope between two or three posts to support a climbing rose. Try the old fragrant pink and apricot Rosa 'Phyllis Bide' or perhaps one of the new 'English Roses' such as the scented crimson 'Tess of the d'Urbervilles' or the beautiful pink 'The Generous Gardener', which will climb, but not overpower everything in sight.

into the secret garden

If you do have the space to create a garden that is for your pleasure alone, how will you enter it? A gate, a battered old door secured by a huge rusting key, elegant wrought iron or a simple archway? Or a path, winding away to the heart of your garden?

Make the path curve away, so although you know what's coming next, you can't immediately see it. That way you'll be surprised, as the seasons change, by new growth, by buds, by seed heads, spiders' webs rimed by dew and frost, the sharp green points of snowdrops and daffodils. Plant only what you really like, not what the garden centre dictates. Tiny cyclamen, precious early *iris reticulata*, single snowdrops, golden aconites, the soft, pale primrose – all flowering at the darkest time of the year. Secret flowers.

'One coloured primrose growing from a clump,

One Lenten rose, one golden aconite,

Dog Toby in his ruff, with varnish bright,

One sprig of daphne, roseate or white,

One violet beneath a mossy stump,

One gold and purple iris, brave but small

Child of the Caucasus, and bind them all

Into a tussie-mussie packed and tight

And envy not the orchid's rich delight.'

Vita Sackville-West, *The Garden*

*A sense of mystery –
what delights lie beyond
the gate?*

18

This moss-covered staddlestone and the carved profile of a young woman add interest and pleasure to a walk around the garden.

Your garden should give up its secrets slowly. Create diversions along the way to make you pause. A solemn figure or an old staddlestone at the turn of the path, a cluster of scented calamint (try *Calamintha* 'White Cloud' or 'Blue Cloud') or a bushy rosemary, lavender or lemon verbena (*Aloysia triphylla*, sometimes found as *Lippia citriodora*) on a sunny corner so that you can brush the scent out with your fingers as you pass. Fill a damp dark space with frondy ferns so that each day in spring you can watch the tender croziers unfurl, bringing green life to a dead place.

Look for roses that bloom very early, such as the single yellow *R. xanthina* 'Canary Bird' and the wonderful soft-scented apricot-pink 'Old Glory Rose', *R.* 'Gloire de Dijon', or those that flower late, as does the climbing *R.* Aimée Vibert, who holds her enormous clusters of white blossoms from August through to October or November. Or plant roses with interest beyond their flowering season like the red-stemmed, grey-leaved *Rosa glauca* or *Rosa moyesii*, whose clusters of large translucent orange-red hips light up the garden for months.

Hunt around reclamation yards for inscribed stone plaques or terracotta carvings that can be fastened to an ivy-covered tree trunk, fence or wall. Cut away the ivy where your plaque is to go, so that it is inset and framed by the leaves that remain.

Interesting plant combinations and unusual garden sculpture give a highly personal feel to any garden.

Be single-minded about choosing the materials and plants that really please you.

A gravelled path overhung with catmint, lady's mantle (*Alchemilla mollis*) and hardy geraniums could be your idea of heaven, but, there again, you might long for brick, edged with tightly clipped box, or stone, lined with pots full of colourful annuals. A well-trodden grass path – edged itself with delicate fronds of flowering grasses, to create a soft green walk to the heart of the garden – is another ideal.

If you opt for gravel, make sure the chunks of stone are not so big that they are difficult to walk on nor so small that they become a nuisance, working their way into other parts of the garden. Pea shingle is perfect, although it will need the occasional rake over to keep a covering in the centre of the path. The bonus for gardeners who like a constant supply of new plants is that seedlings will appear in the gravel, to be left or planted out elsewhere.

Stone and brick paths are both more formal and lend themselves to tidier planting or neat topiary, although their hard edges can be softened with a mat-forming foliage plant such as the woolly *Stachys byzantina* (lamb's ears), a low-growing grey-leaved wormwood (try silvery *Artemesia schmidtiana* 'Nana' threaded through with the improbable-looking 'black mondo grass' *Ophiopogon planiscarpus nigrescens*) or perhaps the tiny, exuberant daisies of the pink- and white-flowered *Erigeron karvinskianus,* which will seed itself with quiet determination into every crack and crevice.

A grass path needs more attention and, unless you make it wide enough not to wear a groove in the middle, is harder to maintain than gravel, brick or stone; but a path of soft turf, leading you on, curving away, can bring back glorious memories of childhood. Who doesn't remember the warm, slightly damp feel of grass as you lay or knelt to peer into flowerbeds, now at eye level? The juicy smell, the overhanging leaves tickling your face, the pattern of squashed grass leaves on your legs as you reluctantly stood up to go back indoors after lying happily in a grassy corner, reading?

Grass on grass might seem a strange way to go about things, but it does work well. Many of the shorter and medium-height grasses create a haze of shimmering silver and pink and gold flowerheads as the light catches them; the slightest breeze gives movement and a whisper of sound.

Plant the frothy pink-flowered *Stipa arundinacea*, the delicate and beautiful silver-tressed *Stipa tenuissima* and sparky golden *Eragrostis airioidies* along the length of your path. The grasses will look good for most of the year as long as you give them a haircut in very early spring to allow plenty of new growth to come through.

Ornamental grasses give colour and texture throughout the year. They bring a light of their own into a planting.

'There seemed to have been grass paths here and there, and in one or two corners there were alcoves of evergreen with stone seats or all moss-covered flower-urns in them.'

Frances Hodgson Burnett,
The Secret Garden

25

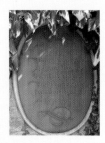

A superb mix of formal topiary and informal underplanting leads you on to a treasure at the end of the path.

'Being led up the garden path' implies that you've been deceived, bamboozled or hoaxed – which is a shame, as any good path ought to be a bit of a tease and should lead you on, but then must deliver something at the end.

Who would mind being led up the garden path to find a sunny arbour, a bed of sumptuously scented herbs, a pretty pool or a shaded seat? Or, as in this section of an enclosed garden, to be brought face-to-face with an oval of Portland stone fastened to an ivy-hung wall? The inscription reads:

'Amidst ye flowres

I tell ye houres

Tyme wanes awaye

As flowres decaye

Beyond the tombe

Fresh fflowrets bloome

Soe men shall ryse

Above ye skyes.'

Shady steps are edged with a mix of hardy ferns. Echeveria (above) are happy outside in the summer but must have protection from frost.

Creating different levels in a garden provides the same sort of glorious anticipation created by a curve in a path. Climb up a flight of steps and you expect to be rewarded with a view, a terrace, an opening out, perhaps a seat. Walk down and you might stumble across a pool or flowing water, a more enclosed space.

Most garden steps are made of brick or stone, although battered old railway sleepers, cut to length and given depth with an infilling of earth topped with gravel, are popular.

The width of your flight of steps, the angle at which it is set, whether it is straight or curved, can create very different effects. Pairs of pots, filled with upright, spiky or exotic plants, could be lined up at either end of wide steps. Use dark-leaved cannas, or agapanthus, clivia, phormium or cordyline, set two by two for a formal effect, if the steps follow a straight line – a curve in the flight will narrow the perspective and lessen the impact of the plants. Or place pots of plants just on the bottom one or two steps – fill low pots with black pansies, tiny yellow daisies, or plant up shallow dishes with subtly coloured echeveria.

Of course there's no need to use steps as pot stands unless you want to – hide the joins with edge-softening plants that will spill gently from step to step. Shady steps look good with a low carpet of ferns.

treasures of a secret garden

Who could resist following a narrow path bordered by fat round green heads of box atop thin stems? They stand, friendly sentinels, urging you on. The other side of the path is lined with a low, neatly clipped hedge.

Topiary, the art of clipping evergreen plants into geometric or figurative shapes, came here with the Romans, who apparently liked to use it as a kind

Clipped shapes give a pleasing structure and add perspective along the ground and at eye level.

of signature at the front of their grand villas, spelling out the names of owners. Tightly clipped hedges, lines of perfectly shaped standard box, yew trees turned into giant chess sets, are found in many gardens in mainland Europe and – increasingly – here in England. A secret garden, where you may enclose box or euonymus with tidy hedges to make a design within a design, is the perfect setting. Use it to give height and definition to a border of otherwise low-growing plants, or to draw the eye along the length of a path to a fountain, sculpture or urn, the perfect geometric shapes bringing a sense of harmony and balance.

It is possible to buy frames to shape your box or yew tree, but those who are in the know say it is best to do it – patiently – by hand and eye. Clip little and often, using scissors and secateurs, between May and September.

Cats can be perfect companions, enjoying a secret garden as much as their owners.

The ancient Egyptian god of pleasure, love and joy was Bast, represented as a cat. The sensual pleasure afforded by a secret garden – sun-warmed places to sleep, small animals to toy with and deliciously scented plants to roll in – can add up to cat heaven.

The cat, being a very self-contained, secretive creature, allows us to provide the things he enjoys and does exactly as he pleases. It is interesting how many owners of highly individual gardens choose real or representational cats as the spirit of the place.

Stone cats lie curled up on steps and among flowers. Pottery cats guard their corner of the garden while real felines prowl the whole territory, regarding strangers with a wary eye. The owner of one jewel-like small garden, full of unusual varieties of well-grown plants, perfectly placed pots and a very pretty pond, regards her 'lounging cats' as a great part of the garden's charm.

Cats have their routine and their territory. If they want to curl up on your garden chair or lie on seed trays in the greenhouse, there's very little you can do to stop them. So just give in gracefully and your cat might stop regarding you as an interloper in his or her garden. Plant plenty of catmint for your pleasure and for feline sensual delight and enjoy the garden together.

Naked ladies dancing brazenly in the borders or a chubby cherub clutching a jar in one hand and making sure his modesty is intact – just – with a piece of cunningly carved cloth. A bizarre bronze head poking out of the border with a neck frill of antirrhinum and calamint or a gleaming stainless-steel dragonfly anchored to the ground with a thin metal spike but looking just as if he's about to take flight, a giant among midgets. Which one will you choose?

Some will say that the shape, colour and texture of the plants in a garden, perhaps some topiary and an urn or sundial as a focal point, is enough. Too much fun or classical allusion or interpretation of nature detracts from the real picture.

Others enjoy the space and freedom to indulge their passion for cats or frogs, strange stone heads, odd pieces of sculpture or even pieces of much older stonework 'rescued' from redundant churches or reclamation yards. Some people are inveterate snappers-up of unconsidered trifles, unable to resist poking around junk shops in the hope of finding something that little bit different to hide away in their gardens.

Bizarre can be quite
beautiful – garden
ornaments are a matter
of personal taste.

Small stone or lead animals, jokey plant supports and carefully arranged piles of pebbles or stones can be placed almost at will in your garden. If it pleases you to make your dragonfly sculpture soar over light-filled grass, then that's the place to put it.

From the classical to ultra modern – this stone cherub looks wonderful in a formal setting, while the stainless-steel dragonfly sits gracefully against a backdrop of ornamental grass and sea holly.

But the larger pieces – sculpture or statues or imposing urns – need careful placing at the ends of paths, tops of steps, to lighten a dark corner or to draw the eye thus far, so that you enjoy what you see, disregarding the wall or hedge beyond.

It's no good going out to buy a 'garden statue' to order. You'll almost certainly end up with something horrible in the wrong place. Wait until you find your putto, cherub or cupid – perhaps in an auction room, in a junk shop or in a reclamation yard. Or you might be moved by something more modern – a simple figure or a large piece of polished stone.

Imagine the piece surrounded by spring flowers, green summer growth, rimed by sparkling frost. Will it be the right piece in the right place and, more to the point, will it lift your spirits every time you walk past?

Abstract pieces of pottery, sculpture and so-called 'garden installations' can be arranged in such a way that they fall into a rhythm that is at once soothing and stimulating. It takes a bit of courage and imagination to 'plant' these African musical notes, made of clay, so that they sing along the top of a high beech hedge in a calming horizontal line. Potter Jonathan Garratt displays this 'Afrikmisik' in his Dorset pottery garden on the right-hand side of an opening in the hedge. On the left is a kayak, found abandoned, paint peeling and earth-bound, an evocative reminder that redundant objects can still have a purpose and a beauty.

Very small and secret are these conical clay 'toadstools', their soft grey caps shining with the same light that strikes the stripy green grass around them. The quiet pieces await the small creatures – mice, voles, ants and snails – that will surely visit them during the course of a day and a night and not be seen by any human being at all.

Garden sculptures in perfect rhythm with their surroundings. The musical notes and the conical toadstools are made of clay.

39

A brick pedestal is a good base for this formal urn (above). The free-flowering pelargonium (centre) would be happy in any well-drained container. Hand-thrown terracotta pots (far right) will fit in anywhere.

Seeking out containers for plants can be fun. It takes a bit of imagination to translate an old rain-hopper or a wire chicken feeder into something that you use to show off small trailing sedum or cobwebby sempervivum, but once you start hunting you'll see possibilities in all sorts of objects that started life as something else entirely. Given good drainage, even old fluted galvanized-iron washtubs will make good homes for a medium-sized shrub – perhaps *Abelia x grandiflora* or *Indigofera heterantha*.

Some plants, such as the lovely grey-leaved, blackcurrant- and pistachio-flowered sage, *Salvia discolor*, look best displayed on their own in a traditional tall urn or large chimney pot. Old-fashioned regal pelargoniums such as Lord Bute, with his deep velvet ripe-raspberry and silver petals, are quite imposing enough to be planted in an elegant urn or stone pot.

Reclamation yards packed out with period architectural cast-offs, cathedral workshops, auction rooms, even junk shops, are all excellent hunting grounds for special containers. There's a good chance that you'll also find a suitable pedestal or stone or brick support for raising the display from the ground.

Whatever you choose, make sure there's a hole in the container to allow water to drain away and that a layer of broken crocks or stones fill the space between the bottom of the pot and the compost to ensure that the roots don't become waterlogged.

Somewhere near you there's a man or a woman making garden pots by hand. They'll be using traditional methods and materials but they will each have their own style and design, making each of their pieces unique. These craftspeople use locally dug clay, maturing and softening it over many months before throwing, glazing and firing their pots and bowls.

Pots made like this are distinctive, durable and frost-proof. They're worth seeking out because of the quality of the workmanship that goes into their

making. The potters who work in this way are highly trained and very skilled artists who have decided to use natural materials. The earth, which sustains all plant life, is carefully transformed by the craftsman's hands into an object at once beautiful and useful – and still capable of nurturing plants.

Choose wide shallow bowls for alpines, sempervivum, succulents – plants that don't need much moisture. Tall narrow-based pots are best for a plant that will drape itself elegantly over the sides, while a fat-bellied pot can hold large plants without fear of being bowled over by gusts of wind. Look around and you'll be amazed at the creativity of many potters – you'll see pots to sink into the ground, triangular 'pocket' pots and upside-down pots to place over the top of a graceful grass so that it 'grows' through the hole in the top.

There's a pot for every plant. A good potter will make a range of tough garden pots from the sublimely classic to the frankly funky.

A dovecote is a pretty feature in its own right, but it is not impossible – with some time and patience – to introduce a few white fantails to your garden. The time and patience is spent on the first pair, who need to be kept captive inside their new home for about six weeks. During this time they'll grow accustomed to their surroundings, and to each other.

A little time and effort and you could be rewarded with the sight and sound of white doves in your garden. A pair is all you need to start your colony.

There are few sounds as wonderfully soothing as the gentle purring and low grumbling of doves as they sun themselves on a warm afternoon. The soft, drowsy cooing and murmuring of white fantails is the very essence of an English summer's day.

'The moans of doves in immemorial elms
And murmuring of innumerable bees …'
wrote Tennyson, who had clearly felt his eyelids drooping irresistibly as he sat in the garden, listening to the sleep-inducing sounds.

The heart-stopping moment comes when one – generally the male – is released to make a reconnaissance flight and return to his mate. Once that is successfully accomplished, the pair will bill and coo away and more white doves will be born in fairly rapid succession. In summer they'll lounge around, cooing gently and soaking up the sun; in winter the sight of a squadron of white doves, wheeling and turning against the dark skies, will take your breath away.

Hurdles made of coppiced hazel, fencing panels woven out of flexible willow, plant-support pyramids and obelisks of these materials all have their place in a secret garden.

Use the hurdles and panels as windbreaks or to achieve shelter and privacy, but consider what you will plant in front of them. This willow fence panel in an Oxfordshire garden forms an elegant background for a tall pink Japanese anemone. Veronicastrum, delphiniums, late flowering aconite, echinacea, agapanthus, some of the taller slender grasses such as miscanthus or calamagrostis would all look good.

Hurdles, with their darker rustic texture, stand well behind shrubbier subjects – perhaps a variegated holly or a euonymus, a small bright-leaved philadelphus or a wonderfully dramatic late-flowering display of the tall golden *Rudbeckia* 'Goldsturm'.

Wigwams such as the one below, with a cheerful black-eyed Susan (*Thunbergia alata*) scrambling around it, are best kept for summer use only. Allow very tender plants such as the thunbergia or the lovely blue morning glory vine (*Ipomoea indica*) to smother it during the summer, then bring it under shelter during the worst of the winter weather. A group of three or five wigwams supporting old-fashioned highly scented sweet peas would make a stunning addition to a potager or summer border.

Windbreaks, fences, pyramids and obelisks, made from indigenous materials such as hazel and willow, give a natural look.

Each garden has a secret life of its own. Underneath the water in your pond, in tree branches, in the shrubs and in the climbers on the wall, scurrying along the soil and hidden in cracks and crevices are legs and fins and beaks and wings. Heartbeats and wing beats, murder and new life. Creatures that crawl, scurry and creep, creatures that fly, burrow and swim. We see only a tiny part of what goes on and, if we are able to act the part of silent watchers, we will find our own lives enriched by the daily drama of other creatures.

This abundance of wildlife can be nurtured by planting pollen- and nectar-rich flowers for bees and butterflies, cutting down on the use of poisonous chemicals and providing water and shelter for small animals.

Watch the bees and butterflies cluster round thistly plants like echinops (globe-thistle), globe artichokes and eryngium (sea holly). They love sedum and angelica, too, as well as fennel, catmint, tobacco plants and verbena of all sorts, from the tall *V. bonariensis* to the tender annual bedding types. Don't be too hasty to tidy up in winter – allow seed heads to remain for the finches to feed on and leave safe places where visiting hedgehogs can curl up for their hibernation.

A pond – even if it is only a small one – will bring a new layer of life to the garden. Certainly birds will swoop down to drink, but beneath the surface of the water there will be the stirrings of newts and frogs, dragonflies and damselflies will dart around to lay their eggs, and all manner of tiny creatures will take up residence.

Entertainment value is not the only benefit – the bonus of encouraging natural wildlife is a balanced and beautiful garden.

Fennel and globe artichokes are two of the many pollen-rich plants beloved of bees and butterflies.

in harmony with a secret garden

'I cannot see what flowers are at my feet

Nor what soft incense hangs upon the boughs,

But, in embalmèd darkness, guess each sweet

Wherewith the seasonable month endows

The grass, the thicket and the fruit-tree wild;

White hawthorn, and the pastoral eglantine;

Fast-fading violets cover'd up in leaves;

And mid-May's eldest child,

The coming musk-rose, full of dewy wine,

The murmurous haunt of flies on summer eves.'

John Keats, *Ode to a Nightingale*

A comfortable seat surrounded by flowers is where you can lose yourself in quiet contemplation.

Why is it so difficult simply to be? To exist but not to do? To be conscious of yourself and all that is around you but without wanting to move or to change or do anything at all? Be determined when you devise your secret garden to have at least one place to sit or lie. And make sure your seat is comfortably placed where you feel you might be able to sit for a while, emptying your mind of all its doing concerns so that you can concentrate on being.

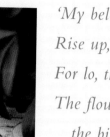

White seats can work perfectly if they are set in the right places.

'My beloved spake, and said unto me,

Rise up, my love, my fair one, and come away,

For lo, the winter is past, the rain is over, and gone.

The flowers appear on the earth, the time of the singing of
the birds is come, and the voice of the turtle [dove] is
heard in the land.

The fig tree putteth forth her green figs, and the vines with
the tender grape give a good smell.

Arise, my love, my fair one, and come away.'

From *The Song of Solomon*, The King James Bible (translated 1611)

White seats can ruin the harmony of a garden, say the designers. And, in many instances, so they do, overpowering the gentle colours, shouting 'look at me', relentlessly white. But there are places, at the centre of a formal grouping, in a white garden, and hidden right away in a shady corner, where they look absolutely perfect.

These three white seats are all tucked in secret corners of the same garden. Two are overhung by fig trees, so that in August you can sit, reach up and pluck a ripe fig as you contemplate the maturing garden. The other is barely visible with its overmantle of clipped *Choisya* – there's just enough room for one to sit.

I'll tell you how the sun rose,
A ribbon at a time.
The steeples swam in amethyst,
The news like squirrels ran.

The hills untied their bonnets,
The bobolinks begun.
Then I said softly to myself,
That must have been the sun!

Emily Dickinson,
I'll tell you how the sun rose

An opened book, a sunhat left on an abandoned chair. Where is the reader, the hat-wearer? Will he or she return to finish the chapter, enjoy the rest of the quiet afternoon?

A lone seat set in the garden, its position, the materials with which it is made, all give clues to the person who uses it. A comfortable seat in the shade denotes a reader, a person who comes out to think, while a wooden bench in the sun, surrounded by bright flowers, belongs to someone who wants to breathe in the moment, enjoy the warmth and the colour.

A stone seat, traced with lichen and planted in the midst of thick lavender and rosemary, fruity-leaved salvias and lemon verbena, is used by a dreamer who enjoys the warmth of the old stone and is lulled by the pungent scent into a delicious fantasy. A seat in an enclosed courtyard – gravelled ground,

pots of flowers, walls to provide shelter from a bracing wind – belongs to the sort of person who likes to be outside as often as possible, taking every opportunity to drink their morning coffee or afternoon tea, eat lunch, read, scribble notes, in their garden.

If there were space enough and time, an ideal garden would have seats for all seasons and all moods.

A chair in dappled shade is the place for peaceful reading, while the courtyard bench and table can be used for eating and writing as well.

55

A real luxury would be a seat for each time of day or for special times of the year. Be ready for that moment when the apple or cherry blossom opens, or the first rosebuds break.

Position your chair where you'll see the water in the pond play reflections of light and shade onto a nearby tree trunk, or where overhanging plants are themselves reflected in the water. Look for a place to sit where you'll capture the last rays of the evening sun or the first warmth of morning.

The elevation of the seat can be important too – you might like to look down on the garden if you have a piece of high ground; on the other hand, an eye-level view through a tangle of soft colours could be equally pleasing.

Your garden might simply be a seat and a window box – but you should still sit and watch.

Sit where you are able to watch the natural life of the garden.

'*Look at Gethsemane as a window box,*
And in that matutinal torchlight and shadow
The cup of suffering's a cup of water

Running among stones and wildflowers,
The secateurs a good substitute for the sword-
Edge. Dead-heading or re-seeding, marl-

Fingered, begin it clear-headed, stippled
With light, self-possessed as a herm watching
The watchful, cocked head of a sparrow,

A purgatory of aimless winds, the pollen-
Dust a tithe gathered on the legs of worker-bees
Earthbound for once, but only, only just.'

Toby Rivas, *The Window Box*

Shelter, colour and scent are all offered by this sitting place in the centre of a small garden.

Virgin's Bower is the old English name for clematis, the best-loved climber of all. It's just the plant for your own bower or arbour, the place where you sit when you need shade or shelter.

A secret bower in the heart of the garden should be surrounded by fragrant flowers, so that you look out on your world through a fretwork of sweet-scented colour and shape. This simple arbour in the heart of a small garden has an elegant open wooden framework and a light canvas roof. It is airy enough for a view of the garden but with the strength to support two beautiful clematis. The first, *C. triternata*

rubromarginata, with its hazy cloud of deep pink and white starry flowers, blooms in profusion from July through to the end of September, throwing its mantle at least twelve feet. As the sun warms the petals, the air is filled with the scent of sweet almonds. Its partner, the fluffy-headed *C. viticella* 'Purpurea Plena Elegans', of a soft violet-purple, scrambles up another panel.

The arbour is surrounded by silken-petalled poppies and hardy geranium in the summer while, later, the deep pinks, blues and orange hues of ice plant, michaelmas daisies, sneezeweed and coneflowers form a flowery fence.

the rhythms of a secret garden

Apples left to ripen on the trees and a basket full of home-grown produce are seasonal pleasures.

We've come this far into our secret garden, but have we thought what we want both to give and to get from it? We've considered the tranquillity, the restfulness of a garden and our own desire to use it as a place to forget the stresses and pressures of life outside. But what can't be forgotten is the toughness of nature, its ability to look after itself, the eternity of it. To be a gardener is to work with the seasons and the natural cycles of life, not to try to fool them or fight them.

The proper pleasures of fruit and flowers in their own season are something we're rapidly forgetting as produce is jetted in from all over the world and, without a second thought, we buy tulips in the autumn and roses at Christmas. Let your garden reflect the natural rhythm of things and enjoy the seasonal pleasures as they come and go. One bright spidery scented sprig of witch hazel (*Hamamelis mollis*) or spicy wintersweet (*Chimonanthus praecox*) or the deliciously fragrant winter honey-suckle (*Lonicera x purpusii*) to enjoy in the depths of winter is worth one hundred scentless imported roses.

'Where is Heaven? Is it not
Just a friendly garden plot,
Walled with stone and roofed
* with sun,*
Where the days pass one by one
Not too fast and not too slow,
Looking backwards as they go
At the beauties left behind
To transport the pensive mind.'

Bliss Carman, *Where is Heaven?*

The first tiny new potatoes, baby carrots, sweet tomatoes, a handful of runner beans are eagerly anticipated. Growing fruit and vegetables on a small scale, among flowers, in pots and in a potager, each bed neatly edged with box, is entirely possible.

In fact carrots grown in large pots often mature more quickly and with less pest damage than those sown in the ground. The carrot-root fly, whose larvae nibble away at the growing roots, can only fly up to about twenty inches. If your carrots are grown at this height, the fly can't lay its eggs among the crop. As soon as you have roots of edible size, start pulling them to allow the others to swell. Continue sowing throughout the season for a constant supply. The first early new potatoes can also be grown in big tubs. There's a satisfaction, when you think that they might be ready, in simply working your hand down to the root, feeling for some perfect white egg-sized tubers.

Runner beans with their beautiful red, purple or red-and-white flowers can wind their way up supports in the flower borders or stand alone with perhaps an underplanting of dark-leaved tree spinach (purple orache or *Atriplex hortensis*) or a cloud of orange and yellow marigolds, which ward off damaging aphids.

Vegetables such as these plump, pretty runner beans add to the beauty and variety of a garden.

63

*Growing edible produce
in small ornamental
beds is practical as well
as pretty.*

Growing vegetables and herbs on a small scale means you can seek out some of the lovely old equipment used by the Victorian gardeners to protect their early crops from predators and frosts. Old lantern lights, rhubarb jars and bell cloches all have their place in the garden – use them to protect early lettuce and other seedlings from sudden drops in temperature and from raids by slugs and snails.

Be creative with shape and colour by growing salads and herbs in a series of small box-lined beds. Alternate rows of frilly dark-leaved lettuce with a soft green variety, plant sweetcorn through feathery dill, grow 'chequerboards' of red radish and white salad onion.

Outline the beds with herbs – chives, marjoram, thyme and parsley all make good 'edgers'. Plant a few ornamental onions for extra interest – *Allium cristophii* looks spectacular for months as its seed head remains intact, and the taller Allium *'Purple Sensation'* is, as its name suggests, a lovely colour.

water in a secret garden

Water changes everything in a garden. Add even a trickle splashing over pebbles, a tiny pool, a basin with water reflecting the sky and trees, a pond or a gently flowing stream and you introduce tranquillity and a subtle change of pace.

We instinctively move towards water, recognizing our need for it on many levels. Life would not be able to exist without water, and it is the central force in many human ceremonies around the world, from simple feet-washing rituals to baptism.

Lie down and peer into an ordinary garden pond. It teems with life from terrifying-looking dragonfly larvae to pond-skaters and silvery upside-down water boatmen scooting across the surface. There are snails, probably fish, possibly newts (shine a torch into your pond at night and you might see them), frogs (tadpoles in the spring) and a host of other tiny creatures, all occupied with completing their life cycles successfully. There's birth, death and even murder going on in your pond, all part of the balance of nature.

Even the busiest of us will slow down to gaze into a pool, stop to listen to the urgent rush of a stream or become mesmerized by the gentle trickle of water over stones, flowing from a simple bamboo pipe.

This semi-formal pond in a small town garden supports a variety of wildlife, from frogs and newts to dragonflies and damselflies.

Imagine a perfectly square pond cut out of roughly mown grass, no hard edges, water up to the brim. Nothing in the water but reflections of the sky and clouds. One small tree near a corner of the pool, shading a single chair. Very simple, uncluttered and the perfect place to sit and think – or perhaps just to sit. A gentle scene such as this, which exists in a French garden, might not be everyone's vision of the perfect setting for an ornamental pond, but it illustrates perfectly the attraction of water. That chair beneath the tree is rarely without an occupant.

You don't need elaborate plantings and landscaping to enjoy the sound and sight of water – the two constant trickles illustrated here each feed stone basins. One is set, pool-like, in the ground surrounded by self-sown hardy geraniums and *Hydrangea* 'Annabelle'. The water dribbles out gently from a carved stone vessel, trickling down its pedestal into the tiny pool whose surface reflects the shapes of the leaves and flowers. Stains on the stone mark the constant flow. The other spills into an old moss-covered animal feeding trough by way of an ancient font and carved head. The frog is a reminder of the fun and enjoyment to be had in a garden, as well as the peace and beauty.

Water, trickling gently into stone basins, brings sound and life to a garden.

> '*Now folds the lily all her sweetness up,*
> *And slips into the bosom of the lake …*'

Alfred, Lord Tennyson, *Sonnet*

Formal or given over to nature, plain or embellished, ponds have been giving pleasure to people for centuries. The romance of water, essential to all forms of life, appeals to our senses – the plashing of a fountain, the trickle of a stream, the silvery light of morning playing on the surface, deep shadows in dusky corners, the silky feel of cool water on hot skin. It calms and soothes. So no wonder a pond or a fountain is often at the heart of the garden.

Formal ponds are perfect for showing off water lilies or for surrounding with beds packed with roses and lavender.

A formal pond, edged with brick or stone and with a central fountain, is more often associated with traditional plantings – water-lilies in the pool and perhaps lavender and old-fashioned roses, their heads heavy with richly coloured and sweetly scented petals, planted near by. You might find a neatly clipped low box hedge around a formal pond. The shape is regular – round, rectangular or square – and there will be some uncluttered space to walk around the margins and, very likely, somewhere to sit. Shells, small stone figures, fish or simple spouts sending gentle falls of water into the pool are usual in a formal pool. The splash and trickle of water is as soothing as a gentle lullaby and it also serves the practical purpose of replacing lost oxygen for any fish.

Any pond will attract all types of amphibians, insects, molluscs and birds, but some will do so more than others. If you allow the edge of your pond to merge into a marshy area, you'll be able to grow a great range of plants that provide nectar and shelter. A gradual path into the water makes it much easier for frogs to clamber in and out, while you'll see dragonflies and damselflies darting from plant to plant.

Make sure about a third of the surface of the water is covered with the leaves of aquatic plants such as water lilies, water soldiers (*Stratiotes aloides*) or the blue-flowered pickerel weed, *Pontederia cordata*. This helps keep the water clear by preventing the growth of algae and again provides shelter for fish and frogs.

The unusual fountain in this small pond keeps the water fresh while the plants support a network of wildlife.

If you like a green and secret place, plant rhubarb-like rheum, large-leaved ligularia and grassy sedges on the marshy margins. The latter come in all colours and sizes, ranging from the silvery fountain-like *Carex* 'Frosted Curls' to the taller, red-bronze-leaved *Carex buchananii*. If there's enough shade in your garden, plant ferns like the small and delicate metallic-looking Japanese painted fern (*Nipponicum pictum*), the strappy-leaved hart's tongue fern (*Asplenium scolopendrium*) or the tall and imposing royal fern (*Osmunda regalis*) with its exquisite spring and autumn colouring.

Hostas like a slightly damp shady spot and, if you've successfully attracted frogs and toads into the pond, you should have no damage from slugs and snails.

in conclusion

'What is this life if, full of care,
We have no time to stand and stare?
No time to see in broad daylight
Streams full of stars, like skies at night
A poor life this if, full of care,
We have no time to stop and stare.'

W.H. Davies, *Leisure*

There was a time when the word 'stress' applied only to aeroplane wings and architects' reports on buildings. Now the entire human race seems to be suffering from some kind of stress and the word has become one of the most overworked in the language.

Life follows natural rhythms – day and night, phases of the moon, the seasons themselves, which bring about enormous natural change. We've made our lives more comfortable by turning night into day, winter into summer. But we pay for those extra hours with more work, responsibility – and stress.

Sometimes, for sanity's sake, it is good and necessary to step outside and pause to consider how things work in the real world, where plants obey the signals given by nature. Most grow as daylight hours lengthen, setting up a support system for the small animals, birds and insects in the garden. They respond to the cold, dark days of a long winter by shutting down their systems, storing energy for regrowth when nature tells them the time is right.

It would be sad to think that there was no going back for us. One way to get in touch once more with natural patterns and to lose some of that stress is to make gardens, cultivate plants and vegetables and learn to accept patiently what nature will give to us in the right time and season.

Ivy hangs in great knotted ropes from the boughs of a mulberry tree; the sight is timeless and peaceful.

The fruitless thought of what I might have been,
Haunting me ever, will not let me rest.
A cold North wind has withered all my green,
My sun is in the West.

But, where my palace stood, with the same stone
I will uprear a shady hermitage:
And there my spirit shall keep house alone
Accomplishing its age.

There other garden-beds shall lie around,
Full of sweet-briar and incense-bearing thyme:
There will I sit, and listen for the sound
Of the last lingering chime.

Christina Rossetti, *The Three Stages*

Seeking peace and perfection through acute observation of nature is one of the hallmarks of the Victorian poet, Christina Rossetti.

Like many women of her time (she was born in 1830 and died 64 years later), she led a necessarily confined life. But her spirit and imagination roamed at will to define the truth about human existence.

These verses from *The Three Stages* tell us that she looked to nature for spiritual health and enlightenment – destroying any remaining vestige of grand ambition and building instead a place to sit and listen. You can do that in your own secret garden.

Open the way into a secret garden – and find peace and contentment.

useful addresses and gardens to visit

Some of the gardens illustrated in this book are open on occasion or regularly for the National Gardens Scheme. Please see the National Gardens Scheme yellow book for details. They include:

ALDERLEY GRANGE, *Alderley, Gloucestershire. See pages 7, 8, 26, 27, 31, 60, 70, 75, 77.*

CHIFFCHAFFS, *Chaffeymoor, near Gillingham, Dorset. See pages 22 (col. 1), 30, 40, 50, 74.*

CONHOLT PARK, *Chute, near Andover, Hampshire. See pages 9, 11, 48, 49, 52, 53, 62, 63, 68.*

EXBURY GARDENS, *Exbury, Hampshire. See pages 25, 37.*

HILLESLEY HOUSE, *Hillesley, near Wotton-under-Edge, Gloucestershire. See pages 19, 65.*

HIGHNAM COURT, *Highnam, near Gloucester. See pages 17, 29, 36, 51.*

HODGES BARN, *Shipton Moyne, Gloucestershire. See pages 10, 54, 61.*

THE LITTLE COTTAGE, *Lymington, Hampshire. See back cover and pages 14, 15, 16, 28.*

ROOKWOODS, *Waterlane, near Bisley, Gloucestershire. See front cover and pages 21, 33, 55, 71.*

TRENCH HILL, *Sheepscombe, Gloucestershire. See pages 13, 20, 24, 32, 69.*

2 WARREN FARM COTTAGES, *West Tytherley, Hampshire. See pages 58, 59, 72, 73.*

Craftsmen and women include:

HARE LANE POTTERY, *near Cranborne, Dorset,* is where potter Jonathan Garrett makes his unique pots, ornaments and installations. Telephone 01725 517700. See pages *38, 39, 41, 42, 43.*

MICHAEL TURNER, *Lymington, Hampshire,* is an artist making stainless-steel ornaments. He specializes in beautifully crafted insects such as dragonflies. Telephone 07773 220186 *See page 37.*

RICHARD AND SUZANNE KERWOOD, *Aylesbeare, Devon,* own Windrush Willow, making fencing, borders, plant supports, baskets and trellis. Telephone 01395 233669. Their website is www.windrushwillow.com. *See pages 46, 47.*

DENNIS FAIRWEATHER, sculptor, made the 'bearded planter' on page 23. He can be contacted on 01379 852266.

The photographs on pages 12, 56, 64 (small picture) and 76 (by Stephen Robson) and page 57 (by David Hall) are reproduced with kind permission of The National Trust Photographic Library.

The photographs on pages 23, 34, 35, 44, 45, 66 and 67 were taken in the author's garden.

index

acknowledgments

Gardeners are always generous people and we experienced much of that generosity in the course of writing and taking photographs for this book. We would particularly like to thank the following for their help and kindness in allowing us access to the most secret parts of their gardens:

Mr Guy Acloque and the Hon. Mrs Acloque *(Alderley Grange)*

Mr and Mrs K.R. Potts *(Chiffchaffs)*

Professor Caroline Tisdall *(Conholt Park)*

Mr Edmund de Rothschild *(Exbury Gardens)*

Fiona and Jeremy Walsh *(Hillesley House)*

Roger Head *(Highnam Court)*

Mrs C.N. Hornby *(Hodges Barn)*

Peter and Lyn Prior *(The Little Cottage)*

Mrs and Mrs Des Althorp *(Rookwoods)*

Celia and Dave Hargrave *(Trench Hill)*

Louise and Julian Mitchell *(2 Warren Farm Cottages)*

Jonathan Garrett *(Hare Lane Pottery)*

Richard and Suzanne Kerwood *(Windrush Willow)*

Mrs Stella Martin *(National Gardens Scheme county organizer)* gave us invaluable help in our search for garden features.

The author also thanks photographer Neil Jinkerson for his ability to turn seemingly impossible expectations into beautiful photographs.